Watercolour by Rev. William Monck, 4 September 1843.

AN ACCOUNT OF
BELSAY CASTLE

IN THE

COUNTY OF NORTHUMBERLAND

by
Sir Arthur E. Middleton

THE SPREDDEN PRESS
1990

First published privately, 1910.
Reprinted, 1990, with introduction and
additional drawings and photographs,
by
The Spredden Press
Brocksbushes Farm
Stocksfield
Northumberland
NE45 7WB

ISBN Hardback 1 871739 12 8
Paperback 1 871739 13 6

Printed and bound by
SMITH SETTLE
Ilkley Road, Otley, West Yorkshire LS21 3JP

CONTENTS

ADDITIONAL ILLUSTRATIONS
FOR SECOND EDITION

INTRODUCTION TO SECOND EDITION

Belsay Castle has been described as 'beyond question . . . the finest of northern English tower-houses'.[1] As the name 'tower-house' indicates, it had the lay-out of a medieval house fitted into a vertical tower, with the service rooms in the basement, the communal hall at first floor level and the private accommodation above. The origins of such towers are obscure, but they presumably stem from the square stone keeps of the Norman period and reflect the unsettled times in which they were built, providing adequate protection against small-scale attack and demonstrating the dominant role of their owners in local society. Such tower-houses were popular with the gentry in northern Britain from the 14th century, particularly in Scotland where they continued to be built for some three hundred years. In the case of the early towers such as Belsay, defence was passive, relying largely on the thickness of their massive walls but, after the introduction of hand-guns, towers were built with shot-holes covering the main approaches. These became more effective with the introduction of L- and Z- plans, since the projecting wings permitted the siting of shot-holes covering the faces of the main walls of the tower. It also enabled the stair to be sited in the angles between the main block and the wings, thus simplifying internal planning and avoiding the danger of weakening one of the tower angles by the well of a spiral stair. The L-plan provided at least one extra room on each floor, and the Z-plan even more. Principal rooms were provided with fireplaces and garderobes, and kitchens with water shoots, so there was comfort and plenty of accommodation for members of the family and the servants directly involved with their welfare. However, it must always be remembered that the towers rarely if ever stood on their own, although the ancillary buildings, often enclosed within an encircling courtyard wall, have now almost always disappeared.

INTRODUCTION

Within this enclosure would be provision for domestic services such as a laundry on the one hand, and for farm management such as barns and cattle sheds on the other hand. Towers and associated buildings were often rendered over and lime-washed so that they did not present the rather bleak appearance that they sometimes do today.

In modern times tower-houses are easier to comprehend than the major medieval castles of an earlier period, since one can relate the domestic arrangements — servants' rooms, kitchens, public rooms and family bedrooms — to the lay-out of a modern house. On the other hand, one can underestimate the skill with which they were planned and built, given the intricate relationship between stairs and rooms and between the rooms themselves.

Sir Arthur Edward Middleton, 7th Bart (1838-1933), author of this account of Belsay Castle, inherited the title and the Belsay estates on the death of his grandfather, Sir Charles Monck, in 1867. Throughout his life thereafter his first interest was Belsay: the land and its tenants, buildings, gardens and history. Sir Arthur restored the castle in 1896 and it is probable that the work that was to occupy most of the rest of his life, the recording of the 600-year history of the Middleton family, developed out of his interest in the castle building. Certainly the first part of the history to be written was his *An Account of Belsay Castle*. On July 28 1906 he wrote to John Hodgson:[2] 'I am getting together architectural notes on our old castle here, and W. H. Knowles is making plans and sections and Worsnop is attempting photographs, but on the days he has been here the weather has been unpropitious.'[3] These photographs were used to illustrate the first publication of the *Account:*[4] those of the entrance lobby, the north-west and south-west turrets and the Renaissance doorway were replaced, in the book version, by drawings by R. J. S. Bertram.

It is clear that Sir Arthur later intended the *Account* to form

ii

Photograph of the Castle *c.* 1890.

Photograph of Sir Arthur Middleton in front of the Castle, *c.* 1920.

part of his monumental family history which survives in eight uniformly bound volumes dating from 1919 to 1926.[5] In his own corrected copy[6] Sir Arthur appends the following note:

I think that a copy of the account of Belsay Castle should be bound to match the other volumes of the family account and lettered Vol. IV, Part II. The present Vol. IV (which deals with Sir John Middleton V, the presumed builder of the castle) should have Part I added to the lettering both on the back and side.

The *Account of Belsay Castle* was subsequently printed for private circulation in 1910 and *Sir Gilbert and the Part he took in the Rebellion of the North of England* (which forms Vol. 2 of the History) in 1918.

Sir Arthur would have had access to the family records and transcripts of British Museum records and to the researches of the Rev. John Hodgson[7] who had been lent family papers by Sir Charles for his work on the *History of Northumberland*. Unfortunately, Sir Charles's father, Lawrence Monck, as executor of Sir William Middleton, 5th Bart (builder of the Bantam Folly to the west of the Castle) destroyed many of the family records and Sir Charles 'when young and moving from the Castle into the new home in 1817 burnt great quantities'.[8]

However, when his mother died Sir Charles found a note in her hand which suggested to him that he might have a claim to the barony conferred on Sir John Stryvelin by Summons to the Parliament of 1343.[9] Sir Arthur would have read Sir Charles's correspondence, concerning the Stryvelin connections, though he does not seem to have been convinced, until after the publication of the *Account*, that Stryvelin built the major part of the Castle. He apparently did not know of the drawing by William Twopeny[10] of Belsay castle (August 1832)[11] which clearly shows the arms of Stryvelin quartering those of Middleton above the top window on the south wall of the castle.

INTRODUCTION

The question of the dating of the castle occupied Sir Arthur until a few years before he died: his final Memorandum on the subject is dated October 1924 and June 1929.[12] In it he summarises his views on the question and gives details of some of Sir Charles's building work, including the stepped buttress against the west wall of the Castle which 'destroyed a most interesting part of the Castle'. These details were given him by Nicholas White, son of William White, who had been Sir Charles's head carpenter for the building of the Hall, and by Sir Charles himself.

Sir Arthur concludes, on architectural and historical evidence, that there were two periods of building, the first by Sir John de Strivelyn in about 1372 and the second by Sir John Middleton after the death of his mother, Christina (10 March, 1422) and a subsequent exchange of property with his brother, Thomas, made him the first sole owner of Belsay. A settlement, dated 6 November 1421, arranging for the marriage of Isabella, daughter of the rich and well-known Newcastle merchant, Roger Thornton,[13] with Sir John Middleton V, gave him the resources to finish the Castle. One of the stipulations of this settlement was that Roger covenanted to deliver £200 and eight fothers (one fother = 19½ cwt) of lead, 'as soon as it pleases Sir John to receive it', and it seems likely that this was for the castle roof.

In this dating he agreed with the eminent Northumbrian historian, Cadwallader Bates, who dated the tower of Chipchase (which corresponds closely in architectural detail with Belsay and shares with it the mason's mark of an arrow) to the latter half of the fourteenth century and Belsay to 'not before 1371'.[14] He received support for the dating of the second period of building from Hamilton Thompson, author of *The Military Architecture of England during the Middle Ages* (1912) who visited the Castle in October 1920 and considered that 'the number of fireplaces exceeds that usually provided in castles of a similar character built during the fourteenth

century, and from information I have been able to lay before him
. . . puts the date between 1421 and 1430'.[15]

The only surviving document relating to the Castle is the list
of border castles drawn up for Henry V in 1415 in which Belsay is
described as 'Turris de Belsoe'. It is likely that at least part of the
building took place after this date.

A discovery made by Sir Arthur since the publication of the
Account in 1910 was described in a footnote to Vol. IV, p.55b of his
typewritten history. 'I think there is evidence that Sir John Middleton
VI married a third time. In 1921 it became known that there is in
the Herald's College in London an appendix of notes and drawings
of arms observed by William Dugdale in the churches and castles
of Northumberland attached to his visitation of that county in
1666. He records 14 shields blazoned with arms on the walls and
windows of the great chamber in Belsay Castle . . .'. Sir Arthur
intended to illustrate these shields in an appendix to his account.
He adds: 'I think it was Sir John Middleton VI who put up the shield
in Belsay Castle, viz those of his three wives, Thornton, Ogle and
Melton, adding the ancestral shields of his Melton wife. Why? Did
he think that he might have a claim to the estate of Prudhoe Castle
of Maud (née Melton) Countess of Northumberland who had
alienated it to her husband and the Percies?' The surviving paintings,
which are described in the *Account*, were restored by Sir Arthur.

The *Account* is illustrated by the plans of W. H. Knowles, the
drawings of R. J. S. Bertram and the photographs of John Worsnop.

W. H. Knowles (1857-1943) was a Newcastle architect
responsible for the major portion of Armstrong College, now
Newcastle University. He surveyed many buildings, mainly for
publications, especially for the Northumberland County History.
R. J. S. Bertram (1871-1953) was born in Newcastle and was
well known for his drawings and watercolours, especially of old
Newcastle. He published sketchbooks of Newcastle and Durham

vi

INTRODUCTION

and contributed drawings to various volumes of the Northumberland County History. **John Worsnop**, a photographer of Rothbury, Northumberland, worked between *c.* 1903 and 1950, doing local photography on a wide range of subjects, both studio photographs and landscapes.

Michael Apted
Gillian Dickinson
May 1990

FOOTNOTES TO INTRODUCTION

[1] W. Douglas Simpson in 'Belsay Castle and the Scottish Tower-Houses', *Archaeologia Aeliana,* 1940.

[2] J. C. Hodgson (1854-1927), historian and antiquarian, was librarian at Alnwick Castle from 1899 to 1921. He edited the *Northumberland County History* for eight years and was responsible for publishing Vols IV to VII inclusive.

[3] Letter dated July 28, 1906 in copy of *An Account* annotated by Sir Arthur in Newcastle Central Library Local Studies Collection.

[4] In *Transactions of the Archaeological and Architectural Society of Durham and Northumberland,* Vol. V, 1907. Wrongly titled *Journal of the Durham and Northumberland Archaeological Society* in Sir Arthur's prefatory note.

[5] *Account of the Family of Middleton of Belsay in eight volumes* by Sir A. E. Middleton. Northumberland County Record Office ZM1/S 78/1-8.

[6] Newcastle Central Library Local Studies Collection.

[7] Rev. John Hodgson (1779-1845) Vicar of Hartburn and eminent antiquarian and county historian. Amongst his publications were two volumes on Northumberland and Westmoreland in Britton and Brayley's series on *The Beauties of England and Wales*; a revision of the second edition of *The Picture of Newcastle* (1812); an *Account of Felling Colliery Explosion* (1813); many contributions to publications of the Society of Antiquaries of which he was a founding member in 1813; and his own *History of Northumberland* (6 vols, 1820-40).

[8] Letter to J. C. Hodgson, 18 August 1912. Newcastle Central Library Local Studies Collection.

[9] Sir Charles Monck. Memorandum entitled 'Of the Stryvelyn barony and the Stryvelyns'. NCRO, ZM1 B21/XL.

INTRODUCTION

[10] William Twopeny (1797-1873) was born in Rochester, Kent, and was, by profession, a lawyer. He spent his vacations drawing antiquities wherever he happened to be and was well known as an antiquary, collector and architectural draftsman in his lifetime. In 1874, his brother and executor deposited 38 bound volumes of his drawings and notebooks in the British Museum. They comprise a unique record of domestic and church architecture, artifacts and ornament (see Eric Swain: *William Twopeny in Kent*, 1986).

Drawings survive from Twopeny's visits to Belsay in 1827, 1829, 1830, 1832 and 1834. When Swanstead, an eighteenth century house in the park, was being renovated in the 1940s one of Twopeny's visiting cards was found stuck into a window frame. In 1832, the date of the drawing published here, Twopeny also drew at Alnwick, Chillingham, Wallington and Bamburgh. Drawings also exist for monuments at Aydon, Corbridge, Elsdon and Morpeth.

[11] *Drawings of Ancient Architecture* Vol. III, British Museum, Dept of Prints and Drawings. See also J. P. Neale, *Views of Seats* Vol. II, 1819: 'On the south front of the Tower, over the uppermost window, there are carved the arms of Stryvelin quartering those of Middleton. On the oldest part of the house, adjoining the tower, this order is reversed and the arms of Middleton are made to quarter those of Stryvelyn . . .'

[12] 'Memoranda on the date of the building of Belsay Castle', October 1924 and June 1929, NCRO, ZM1 B 20/XIII/2.

[13] His effigy is in St Nicholas Cathedral, Newcastle.

[14] Cadwallader Bates, *The Border Holds of Northumberland*, Vol. I, p. 146 (Vol. XIV of *Archaeologia Aeliana*, 1891). This was the only volume published.

[15] Note in Sir Arthur's hand in Vol IV, p. 34 of his *Account*.

ERRATA AND ADDENDA

As the 1910 text is reprinted unchanged, Sir Arthur's errata and addenda are given below (NCRO, ZM1 B20 XIII)

p. 9, para 2. Insert after '1240' 'a moiety of' (the other moiety belonged to his brother)

p. 10, lines 1-3. We have evidence now which points to the building being begun in 1409 or in 1422 by the Sir John Middleton living at that date. [Sir Arthur subsequently changed his mind again on the dating: see introduction, ed.]

p. 11, line 17. Omit 'peel'

p. 13, last line. For 'those' read 'that'

p. 17, line 4. For 'pointed' read 'arched'

p. 26, para 2. This arrangement of stair and room might have been purposely contrived for defence and to bring under notice any person passing through the rooms. Ross and MacGibbon Vol 1, pp. 7, 192, 251. Clark's *Medieval Military Architecture*, Vol. 1, pp. 136, 149

p. 28, line 16. After 'saltire argent' add: 'This shield must represent or two bars azure, a chief gules for de Manewrs of Etal, quartering vert 3 Squirrels sejant argent for Baxter of Langeton, both in the county of Northumberland (Raine's *North Durham*, p. 212, Papworth, *Ordinary of British Armorials,* pp. 22 and 171).

ACKNOWLEDGMENTS

I am most grateful to Sir Stephen Middleton, Bart, for his assistance in many different ways, and for permission to publish the watercolour by the Rev. William Monck, second son of Sir Charles (frontispiece), the photographs of Sir Arthur and the Castle and Sir Arthur's Glossary of terms which he intended to be read in conjunction with his description of the castle but which, in the event, he never published. The six monochrome paintings of the castle are from a quarto volume containing unsigned nineteenth-century drawings by Lady Mary Monck and others, now in the possession of Mr Brian Swinburne. They are published with his permission. The eight Twopeny drawings are published Courtesy of the Trustees of the British Museum.

I would also like to acknowledge the help of the staff of the Northumberland County Record Office, Newcastle Central Library Local Studies Collection, English Heritage and the Department of Prints and Drawings of the British Museum.

Gillian Dickinson
May 1990

AN ACCOUNT OF
BELSAY CASTLE

BELSAY CASTLE FROM THE SOUTH EAST.

AN ACCOUNT OF BELSAY CASTLE
IN THE COUNTY OF NORTHUMBERLAND
BY SIR ARTHUR E. MIDDLETON, BART.

Belsay Castle Northumberland

PRINTED FOR PRIVATE CIRCULATION

NEWCASTLE-UPON-TYNE
MAWSON SWAN AND MORGAN LIMITED
M.CM.X

PREFATORY NOTE.

———

THIS account of Belsay Castle was written to place on record its architectural and structural details, and was printed in Vol. 5, Part II, of the Journal of the Durham and Northumberland Archæological Society in 1906. It is here revised and reprinted with more numerous illustrations. The plans and sections are by MR. W. H. KNOWLES, F.R.I.B.A., F.S.A., and most of the drawings are by MR. R. J. S. BERTRAM, both of Newcastle-upon-Tyne. The photographs are by MR. JOHN WORSNOP, of Rothbury.

A. E. M.

BELSAY,
    1st June, 1910.

LIST OF ILLUSTRATIONS

LIST OF ILLUSTRATIONS

BELSAY CASTLE

IN the County of Northumberland, about fifteen miles north-west from Newcastle-upon-Tyne, and eighteen miles from the sea, is a group of abrupt hills or crags, formed by the upheaval of sandstone strata into the form called "Crag and tail," the crags facing towards the west. At the tail or eastern end of the largest of these, anciently called Belshowe, *i.e.*, Bels-hill, stands Belsay Castle. Of the date of its building there is neither record nor tradition. It was probably begun in the fourteenth century, though it may not have been completed till the beginning of the fifteenth century.

In 1240 the manor of Belsay belonged to Richard de Middleton, who in 1270 became Chancellor to Henry III. In 1318 his nephew, Sir John de Middleton, forfeited it for rebellion against Edward II, who granted it to Sir John de Crumbewell, Constable of the Tower of London, and Thomas de Baumburgh, the King's Clerk, for their lives. The reversion was afterwards granted by Edward III to Sir John de Strivelyn, one of his generals, who, on account of some relationship not now known, settled it to devolve after his death and that of his wife, Jacoba, upon Sir John de Middleton and Christian, his wife. This Sir John de Middleton must have been of the same family as that of the Middletons who forfeited Belsay, for he bore the same arms. Belsay has remained in the possession of the Middletons to the present day.   It is possible that Sir John de Strivelyn was the person who commenced the building of the Castle.

Viewed from the outside, it is seen that the castle is rectangular in plan ; the walls, which are of good height, have a moulded offset of about three inches at a level a little higher than that of the floor of the first storey, and are crowned at

THE SOUTH BATTLEMENT AND
THE SOUTH EASTERN TURRET.

10

SEALS.

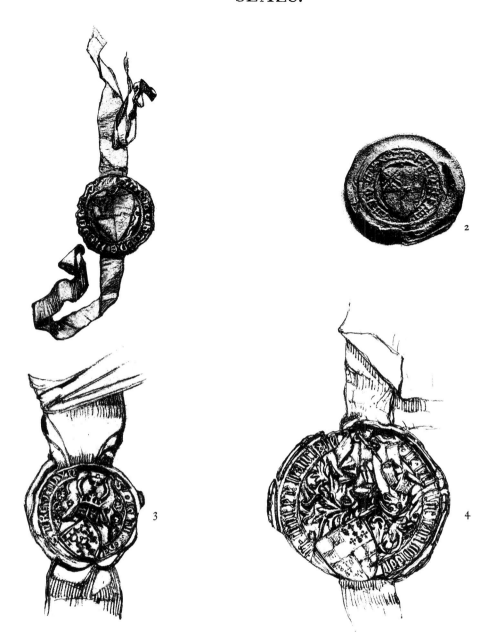

No. 1.—SEAL OF SIR GILBERT DE MIDILTON attached to a receipt given by him to the Episcopal Community at Durham, A.D. 1317. A shield bearing *Quarterly, in the first quarter a stag's head.* Durham Miscellaneous Charters, No. 5053.

No. 2. —SEAL OF THOMAS MIDELTON attached to a deed of exchange of property in Silksworth, Co. Durham, for a moiety of Belsay, between Sir John Midelton of Belsay and Silksworth and his brother Thomas (who owned a moiety of Belsay), April 10, 1422, 10 Henry V. *Penes* W. Grey Robinson, Esq., the representative of the above Thomas Midelton. A shield bearing *Quarterly, in the first quarter a cross.* A cross pattern around in place of an inscription. The heraldic tinctures of the Middleton arms are *Quarterly, gules and or, in the first quarter a cross flory argent.*

No. 3.—SEAL OF SIR JOHN DE STREVELYN attached to a deed in the Durham muniments (1ma 6ta *Spec.* No. 48), 20 July, 35 Edward III., A.D. 1361. A shield bearing *crusilly of cross-crosslets, three covered cups.* Crest : on a helmet, *a covered cup between two bull's horns.* Inscription : "S^i *Johannes de Strevelyn.*" The heraldic tinctures of these arms are *Sable, the crosslets and cups argent.*

No. 4.—SEAL OF SIR JOHN MIDELTON, attached to a deed in the Durham muniments (1ma 6ta *Spec.* No. 43), 4 Nov., 19 Edward IV., A.D. 1479. A shield bearing Quarterly, first and fourth *quarterly without charge* (for Middleton), second and third *crusilly of cross-crosslets, three covered cups* (for Stryvelyn). Crest : on a helmet much mantled, *a savage man* holding a club* (for Middleton). Inscription : "*le seel de Sir John Midelton.*" On the reverse of this seal is a secretum, a double-headed eagle displayed.

* The drawing of this seal incorrectly represents the naked savage man as rather resembling a man in armour.

each corner with a turret. The turrets show semi-circular faces outwards above the external angles of the castle walls, which they oversail on each side in five courses. They do not project beyond the angles, but coincide with them. That the turrets do not oversail the angle is unusual, but another instance is that of Chipchase, where the turrets are similarly placed. Possibly they may have been so treated in order to mitigate the appearance of spreading, produced by optical illusion, at the top of a tall tower. Between the turrets, and placed upon corbels formed of three oversailing stones, are tall machicolated battlements. Low machicolated battlements on corbels also crown the turrets. The south-western turret is attached to a rectangular tower, and both are carried up together to a greater height than the other turrets. This arrangement of a tower and turret of greater height at one corner gives a stately character to the castle, and is unusual in the other Northumbrian peel towers now standing, but it occurs at Cockle Park Tower, and that feature also appears to have existed in the tower of Seghill, which is now partially demolished.*

There was probably a space or barmkin around the castle, enclosed by a strong wall for its further protection, and for shelter for cattle from marauders. There are no remains of this, but in Buck's view of 1728 is shown a ruined building to the south-east of the castle, apparently of strong masonry (as small shrubs and weeds are represented as growing upon it), that may have been a part of these outworks.

* " Seghill Tower consisted of three storeys, with a lofty exploratory turret at one corner, from whence, in clear weather, the Yorkshire coast was clearly visible. The upper part was destroyed in 1827." *Richardson's Table Book, Historical Div.,* vol. III.

BELSAY CASTLE.

The rectangular base of the castle has a length from north to south of 56 feet 2 inches, and from east to west of 47 feet. The walls of the basement storey are on the east side 10 feet

THE ENTRANCE LOBBY
IN THE BASEMENT.

12

BELSAY CASTLE FROM THE NORTH.

William Twopeny: Belsay Castle from the south-east.

and on the north and south 9 feet in thickness, and above this they are of about 7 feet in thickness up to the roof. They are faced on the outside and inside with ashlar work of the sandstone of Belsay hill, the core of the walls being filled with rough stones and lime, forming a hard concrete. This core occupying so large a proportion of the walls, it may be more correct to describe them as being built of concrete faced with ashlar. This concrete is now to be seen where a doorway has been cut through the wall at the northern end of the large room on the basement floor.

The wall on the southern side commences to rise from the ground level with a plinth of 1 foot 9 inches in height, and from the plinth to the underside of the corbels is a space of 43 feet 10 inches, the three stones of the corbels having together a height of 2 feet 8 inches. From the ground level to the top of the corbels is therefore 48 feet 3 inches. The battlement erected on the corbels is 7 feet 2 inches to the top of the merlons, the full height of the wall and battlement being 55 feet 5 inches. From the ground level to the top of the corbels of the south-western tower the wall is 65 feet 4 inches. The battlement erected on this is 4 feet 8 inches, making the full height at this, the highest part of the castle, 70 feet.

When the castle was repaired in 1896 it was found necessary to renew some of the corbels, and on taking off the top of the wall it was found that the uppermost stones of the corbels were more than 6 feet long. This was necessary in order to carry the weight of the machicolated battlements. These vary in height on the several sides of the castle, those on the southern side being 7 feet 2 inches high on the outer face, and giving 6 feet of protection to a man standing on the parapet walk.

On the southern side a cap moulding is carried round the merlons and embrasures, whereas on the other sides of the castle the horizontal surfaces only of the merlons and embrasures are so treated.

It is not likely that the present battlements are those originally constructed by the builders. Where the ends of the battlements meet the sides of the turrets, there are buttresses or shoulders built into the turrets, usually taller and not forming part of the present battlements, which merely abut against them. It is possible that these shoulders were part of the supports of wooden bretesches, which were in early times erected on wooden or stone corbels and supported behind on the walls. Attacking forces learned how to set them on fire, and their use was discontinued, stone battlements being erected in their place upon the corbels. It is a peculiarity of the eastern face of the south-western tower that it has not this buttress. Perhaps this face of the tower may have been rebuilt, or perhaps the change from wooden bretesches to stone battlements may have occurred during the time of its original building.

On the western side of the castle a part of the wall is recessed inwards for a space of 4 feet 5 inches deep by 8 feet 9 inches wide, and in this recess and on the basement level the entrance to the castle is situated. It is a pointed archway 5 feet 6 inches wide and 8 feet high to the crown of the arch, the arch being formed of segmental stones, as are the other door-

LARGE ROOM IN BASEMENT.

ways of the castle, in some instances one stone forming one half
of the arch. The entrance opens into a lobby 9 feet 9 inches by
5 feet 8 inches, on the southern side of which is a doorway into
the staircase, and on the northern side another doorway opening
into a room probably used by the attendant in charge of the
basement. At the eastern end of this lobby an archway 5 feet
wide by 7 feet 5½ inches high, tall enough to admit a horse and
its rider, opens into a large room 38 feet 6 inches by 18 feet
feet 4 inches, with a pointed arched vault, the height being
16 feet 2 inches to the crown of the vault. This room occupies
the whole of the eastern front. It is lighted by two small loops
on the eastern side, and by one on the northern and southern
sides respectively. It was probably used as a kitchen, there
being at the northern end a large fireplace formed by a long
elliptical arch. In the floor towards the northern end is a well,
about 17 feet deep, sunk into the sandstone rock. It is now
dry, owing, perhaps, to the working of a quarry a short distance
away. Part of the southern end of this room was walled off
from the rest, and may have been used as a store. This wall
was removed during the late reparations, as having been no part
of the original construction. As has been already mentioned, a
doorway has been in more modern times broken through the
northern wall, disclosing its concrete interior. Over this room
is the great hall or living room, which, as the outer walls are at
this height about 3 feet each less in thickness, measures 42 feet
9 inches by 21 feet 6 inches. It is 17 feet high. In the eastern
wall, towards the northern end, is a large fireplace, and here
above the salt would be the seats of the lord of the castle and

THE GREAT HALL.

16

Belsay Castle, Northumberland

William Twopeny: **Window in the Great Hall.**

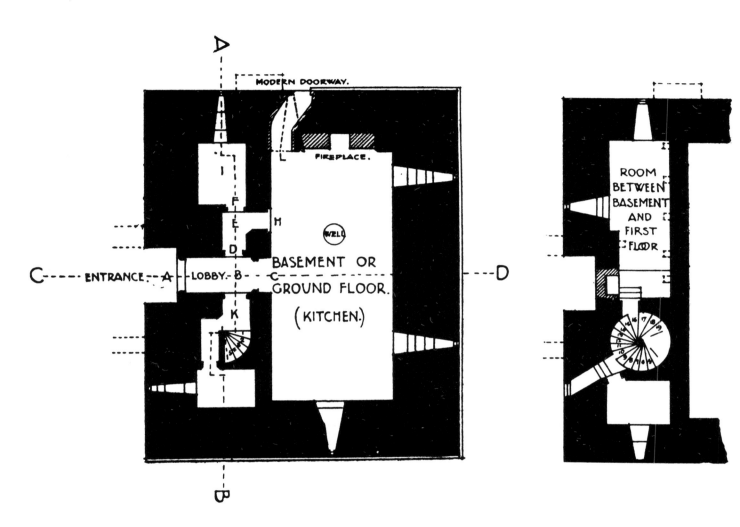

A

MODERN DOORWAY.

L

FIREPLACE.

I

F

E

H

D

WELL

C - - - - ENTRANCE - - A | LOBBY - B - - C

BASEMENT OR

GROUND FLOOR.

(KITCHEN.)

- - - D

K

L

B

ROOM
BETWEEN
BASEMENT
AND
FIRST
FLOOR

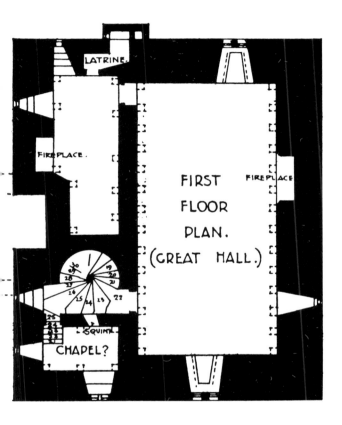

FIRST
FLOOR
PLAN.
(GREAT HALL.)

LATRINE.

FIREPLACE.

FIREPLACE

SQUINT

CHAPEL?

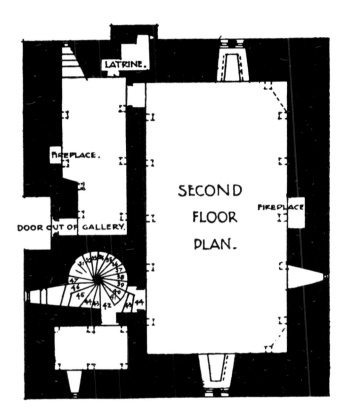

SECOND
FLOOR
PLAN.

LATRINE.

FIREPLACE.

FIREPLACE

DOOR OUT OF GALLERY.

SECOND
FLOOR

FLOOR

ANCIENT
DOOR   FLOOR

GREAT
HALL

FLOOR

LOBBY

SECTION ON LINE C.D. LOOKING NORTH.

CORBELS TO

CORBELS TO

SECTION ON L

ONS.

LOOKING EAST.

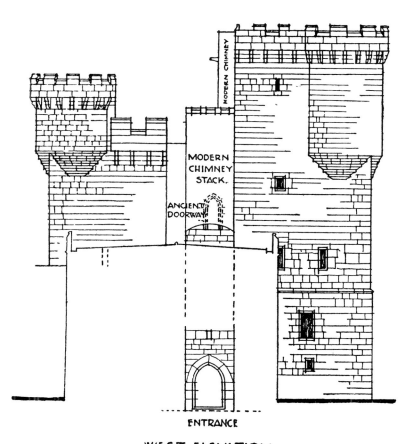

WEST ELEVATION.

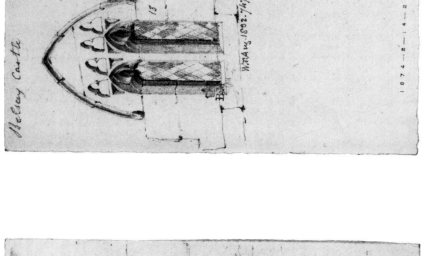

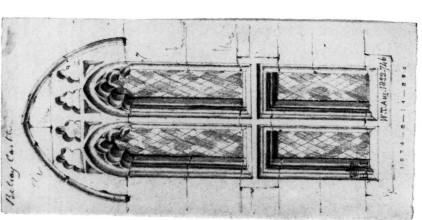

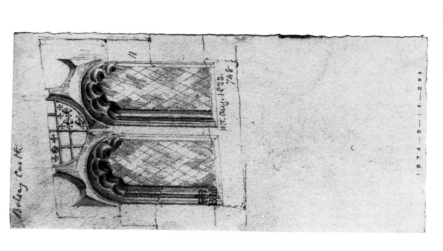

William Twopeny: Details of the windows on the south wall. Note Stryvelin arms quartering those of Middleton.

his family. It is lighted by two windows, one at each end, the northern and the southern, deeply recessed into the walls, with a stone seat on either side. Each window is divided into two lights by a heavy mullion and transom, the pointed tops of the lights being filled with cinquefoil cusping. These windows have had wooden shutters. The bolts for securing them were shot into bosses worked on the mullions. On the outside there is a tympanum constructed of large stones in the form of a pointed arch bearing incised cinquefoils and enclosed by a hood-mould. A good illustration of the interior of one of these windows is given in Turner's *Domestic Architecture of the Middle Ages* (Parker), vol. II, p. 94. There is also a small look-out loop to the east.

Above this room, laid upon rows of stone corbels along each side, was the floor of a room of similar size, but of less height, lighted by two-light windows without transoms, at each end, with cusping the same as in those of the last room, and by a small look-out loop to the east. It is noticeable that none of these windows is exactly over or opposite to the other ; irregularity appears to have been the wish of the architect.

The north-western corner of the castle has on the basement the attendant's room already mentioned, and above that is a room, 24 feet 2 inches by 9 feet 6 inches, opening from the staircase, and lighted by two loops. Above these are two more rooms, one above the other, of the same size, each with a fireplace, making four storeys. The last two have ingress only from the great hall and from the room above it, and none from the stair. In the northern walls of these two rooms, doorways lead into latrines built upon corbels on the outside face of the wall. A portion (10 feet in length) of the southern end of the western wall of these rooms is set back 2 feet 5 inches into the rooms, thus forming a recess 8 feet 9 inches wide by 4 feet 5 inches deep on the outside. This recess continues from the bottom to the top of the castle, the entrance being placed in it on the basement level, as has been above observed. In the western wall of the uppermost of these rooms is a pointed arched doorway opening into the above recess. It apparently

VAULTED ROOM IN
NORTH WESTERN TURRET.

18

DOORWAY OPENING ON TO STAIR FROM GREAT HALL

Belsay Castle Northumberland

W.T. Aug. 1832. 730

1074 — 2 — 14 — 294

William Twopeny: South-western tower and stair seen from the roof.

opened on to a gallery, which may have been constructed of wood, or have been formed by a stone arch, the evidence of which is now destroyed by a stack of modern chimneys built into the recess.

The gallery may have received protection by a bretesche or a machicolated battlement, and may have been used for raising a drawbridge, if such existed in front of the entrance doorway ; or the doorway may have contained a hoist for lifting stores.

NORTH WESTERN TURRET
FROM THE ROOF.

SOUTH WESTERN TOWER AND
STAIR SEEN FROM THE ROOF.

20

BELSAY CASTLE.

In the south-west corner and its tower are six storeys, viz., a small vaulted room on the basement entered from under the stair, and lighted by a small loop. Above this is another vaulted room lighted in the same way. Above this is a room 11 feet 7 inches by 7 feet, and 13 feet 9 inches high. It has a handsome two-light window, the lights having trefoil cusping. In its northern wall, and opening on to the stair, is an opening in the form of a squint, enabling anyone passing down the stair to obtain a view of the east wall of this room and of an altar, if this chamber was used as a chapel, which seems, taking into consideration the ornate character of the window, very possible.

Above this is another room lighted by a loop, projecting from which is shown in Buck's view the dial of a clock, and above this again is a vaulted room, with its lower part in the main building, but having its upper part above the gutter of the roof. As access to this room cannot be got from the stair, it is entered by a door opening from the gutter, and so high in the wall of the room that steps are required to reach the floor 4 feet lower down. This illustrates the inconvenience of a spiral stair which only gives access to rooms on the same side of it on the completion of a revolution.

From the gutter of the roof a stair built into the eastern face of the south-western tower leads to its top. This stair appears to have been at some time in a ruinous condition, as its lower half is now supported by a wall built upon the gutter and awkwardly obstructing part of it. Half-way up, it gives access to a vaulted room, 17 feet 5 inches by 10 feet 9 inches, extending over the last-mentioned room and the staircase, and thus occupying the tower, and completing the six storeys of this corner of the castle. An illustration of this stair is given in Turner's *Domestic Architecture* (Parker), vol. II, p. 13. This room has a fireplace, and is lighted by two loops. Each of the other three turrets contains a vaulted chamber.

Recounting the rooms, there are three storeys of large rooms along the east side of the castle, each with a chimney ; four rooms of medium size in the north-western corner, the two uppermost with chimneys ; six smaller rooms in the south-

VAULTED ROOM IN THE
UPPER PART OF THE
SOUTH WESTERN TOWER.

western corner, with its tower, the uppermost of these with a chimney ; and three chambers in the three other turrets ; making in all sixteen rooms, besides the entrance lobby and staircase, six of the rooms being provided with chimneys.

The staircase is in the northern part of the south-western tower. It is circular in plan, and slightly conical in elevation, being in diameter at the bottom 9 feet 2 inches, and gradually diminishing to 8 feet 5 inches at the uppermost step. It is entered by a doorway in the southern wall of the entrance lobby in the basement, and contains a sinistral spiral stair, *i.e.*, the spiral formed by the ascending stair around the newel passes from the right to the left of a person facing the newel, and as it proceeds around the newel it turns to his right. This is the reverse of the dextral or right-handed screw of the mechanic and of the common corkscrew. A person ascending this stair has his right arm against the newel ; a person descending it has his left arm against the newel, and has his right arm free to use his sword against an attacking party trying to ascend, and at the same time he will be able to shelter himself behind the newel. The stair extends to the roof of the main building, on to which it delivers by a doorway. The newel is 8 inches in diameter. Over the length of the uppermost step is a stone 1 foot 7 inches high, forming a parapet. It is worked at its inner end to coincide with the newel, and is surmounted over this end by a pillar 3 feet 9 inches in height and 9½ inches in diameter, from the top of which eight ribs radiate, after the manner of an umbrella, to support a domical vault. An illustration of this vault is given in Parker's *Glossary*, 5th ed., vol I, p. 325.

VAULTED ROOF
OF STAIRCASE.

24

BELSAY CASTLE.

A similar umbrella vault, supported on the newel of a sinistral stair, in the Warder's tower of Alnwick Castle, is shown in *Illustrations of Alnwick, Prudhoe and Warkworth,* published by the Duke of Northumberland in 1861, and in the *New History of Northumberland,* Vol. V, p. 88, is shown a similar vault over a dextral stair in the spire-turret of Warkworth Castle.

Though it is mentioned above that a sinistral stair gives an advantage in the use of the sword arm to the defenders, yet it is probable that the choice of either form of spiral mainly depended upon the convenience of the access to be given to the rooms opening from the stair. Thus at Belsay the chamber above the basement in the south-western corner could not be entered from a dextral stair. As a spiral stair only gives access to rooms on the same side of it on the completion of a revolution, the arrangement in Belsay of three, four, and six storeys in different parts of the castle made it impossible for any one spiral stair to touch all the rooms on a suitable level for entrance. For this reason the two uppermost rooms of the four-storey tier are entered only from the great hall and from the room above it. In the uppermost of these two is the doorway, already mentioned, opening on to the upper part of the recess over the entrance, evidently an important door, yet only to be reached in so roundabout a way. This inconvenience may perhaps have been mitigated by a series of wooden ladders at the northern end of the second-storey room, at which end there is access to the stair. It has already been observed that the fifth storey of the tier of six is entered from the roof gutter, and requires several steps down from the door to reach the floor. The

architect of Belsay may not have made careful sectional drawings before proceeding to build, and as the work progressed
may have found that his plan of entering three tiers of storeys
differing in height and on different sides of the stair was a
failure.

In MacGibbon and Ross's *Castellated Architecture of
Scotland*, in which a large number of plans of castles are given,
they commonly show a sinistral stair, but in so many instances
there are both dextral and sinistral stairs in the same building,
as, for example, in Inverlochy Castle, vol. I, p. 75, that convenience of access must here again be assumed as the chief reason
for the arrangement adopted.

It has been observed above that the internal arrangement
of the castle is three storeys of large rooms along the eastern
side, four of smaller size in the north-western corner, and six of
still smaller size, with the staircase, in the south-western corner.
These last are roofed by the vaulted top of the south-western
tower, formerly covered with stone flags, and now with Val de
Seyssel asphalt. The two former tiers of storeys had, when the
repairs in 1896 were begun, roofs of low pitch constructed of
cambered oak beams resting on stone corbels, the rafters,
sarking, etc., being of oak covered with lead. The beams had
the appearance of being those of the original roofs, but were
decayed at the ends. The other parts of the roofs were also so
much decayed that the whole was taken down and reconstructed
under the advice of the late Mr. Charles Ferguson, F.S.A.,
of Carlisle.

In the course of this reparation the roof of the large rooms

26

This arrangement of stair and room might have been purposely
contrived for defence and to bring under notice any person passing
through the rooms.

Ross and MacGibbon, Vol. I., pp. 7, 192, 251.

Clark's *Medieval Military Architecture*, Vol. I., pp. 136, 149.

William Twopeny: Vaulted roof of staircase.

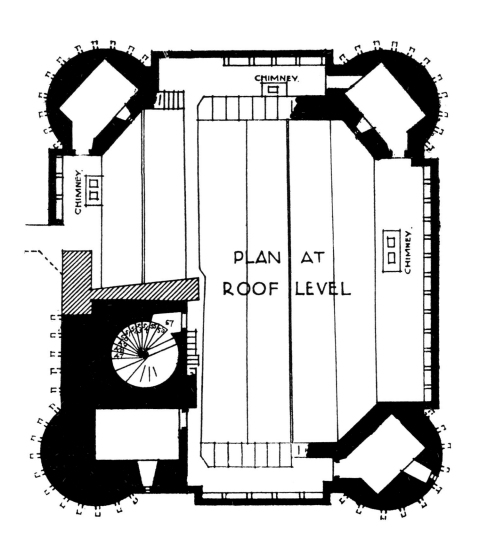

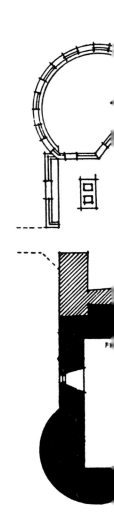

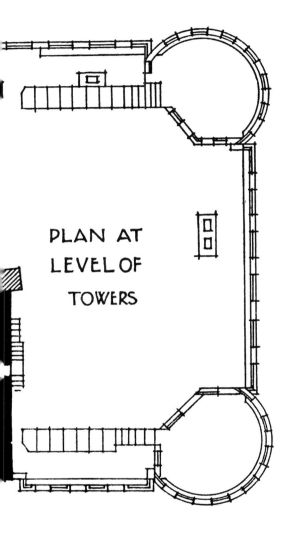

PLAN AT
LEVEL OF
TOWERS

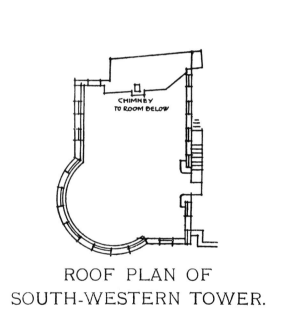

CHIMNEY
TO ROOM BELOW

ROOF PLAN OF
SOUTH-WESTERN TOWER.

on the east side was treated as follows :—First the stone corbels, which were much perished, were renewed where necessary. A course of stone, with a moulding projecting about three inches, was then laid upon the walls between the corbels, and baulks of oak were then laid along the sides of the walls so as to rest partly on the corbels and partly upon the projecting moulding, and by this means the width between the two walls was reduced. Three of the best of the old cambered beams had then the decayed ends sawn off, and were placed with their ends upon the oak baulks, their weight being first upon the baulks, and then distributed upon the moulding and the corbels. Between these old cambered beams were placed two new oak king-post principals, reaching four feet over the outer or eastern wall, and rather less over the inside or western wall, which is not so thick. These two principals are very strong, and make the main supports of the roof. The roof was then covered with new lead, the tops of the walls where exposed being covered with asphalt. It is interesting to state that the roof-tree of the old roof was of oak of one piece, and must have exceeded 42 feet 9 inches, which is the length of the room. Unfortunately, a part of each end was rotten, and had to be sawn off. From the gutters of these roofs the south-western tower, 25 feet 6 inches by 16 feet, rises in height 21 feet 2 inches to the top of its merlons. The three smaller turrets rise about 13 feet 6 inches.

The internal ornament of these mediæval castles was usually mural decoration by painting in colour, and not by carving of stone. At Belsay the walls of the large living room have been so ornamented, though the plaster thus decorated is now nearly all perished away, and the small remains of the painting that are left are now scarcely perceptible. In the splays of the southern window, however, it can be seen that the walls were originally finished with a very thin coat of plaster brushed on with a coarse brush, or perhaps a bunch of birch twigs; and on this plaster has been painted, in a dark red colour, the branches of a vine or other climbing plant. This plaster has, at a later date, been covered with a slightly thicker but still thin coat of plaster carried all round the room. Upon this plaster on the upper four feet of the walls were painted tree trunks with the stumps of lopped branches, on which were hung shields, three only of which could at the time of the reparations be distinguished, viz., a shield bearing *argent a fess between three crescents gules* for Ogle *quartering an orle* for Bertram, a shield bearing *barry of five gules and argent quartering three squirrels*, and a shield bearing *sable a saltire argent*. This latter coat may be that of Sir John de Crumbewell,[*] to whom a life interest in Belsay was given by Edward II as above mentioned. The tinctures of some of the above are doubtful, for the faded colours have been touched over with neutral colour in modern times. The presence of the Ogle shield probably chronicles the marriage of Sir John Middleton to a daughter of Sir Robert Ogle,[†] whose first husband, Sir William Heron, died 1st Sept. 1425. The tree trunks were on a green ground, on which were flowers, the whole reminding us of the pictures in *La Chasse*, by Gaston

---

[*] Papworth's Ordinary of British Armorials.

[†] Other marriages with Ogles were : Thomas Middleton of Belsay, living in the first half of the 16th century, married Margaret, daughter of Ralph 3rd Lord Ogle, and their son Robert Middleton, living in second half of the 16th century, married Mabell, daughter of John Ogle of Ogle Castle.

Remains of Ancient Wall-Painting   (Lower part completed from fragments).

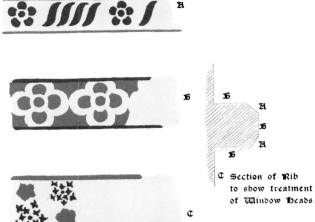

A

B

C

Ornament round Window.

C Section of Rib
to show treatment
of Window Heads.

Shield on North Wall.

Lower South Wall.

Mural Decorations on Wall of Great Hall.

la Foix, published in 1387. This decoration was examined and reported upon by Messrs. F. R. Leach & Sons, of Cambridge, in 1896. See Appendix.

The ceiling of this room has been slightly coved along the sides, and the flat arch thus formed at the southern end over the

REMAINS OF
THE OLD CLOCK.

tree trunks just mentioned showed a naval scene of two ships, with masts and sails and attendant boats. The ships are rudderless, which shows an early date, and the boats are rowed with a paddle. Shields are hung along the side of one of the ships, a Norman custom.

There are the remains of an old clock, the dial of which is shown of a diamond shape, projecting from a small window on the southern front, in Buck's view of 1728. Later, and until taken down, it had a circular dial 4 feet 4 inches in diameter. The clock is made of iron, and mounted on a wooden frame 3 feet 10 inches by 2 feet 11 inches. It was worked by stone weights, and struck the hours on a bell. It was wound by means of handles or spokes projecting radially from one end of each of its two barrels. In its original construction it was not regulated by a pendulum.* Its date was therefore probably before 1621, when the pendulum was first used in England.† This clock may have been erected when the Jacobean additions to the residence were made in 1614.

In the reparations that were made a few years ago, some of the corbels supporting the battlements between the turrets were found to be much perished. On the western wall the northern-most corbel was built in under the wall of a turret, and could not be replaced in that position, and was replaced to the south of the turret wall, and the battlement consequently projects awkwardly beyond it. A similar restoration of a corbel had been made on the north side sometime during the nineteenth century.

---

* It was altered to work with a pendulum about the year 1800.
† *Clocks, Watches, and Bells*, by Lord Grimthorpe, 1903, p. 30.

BELSAY CASTLE.

In the basement plan an interesting question arises. Why was the secondary lobby E (shown on the plan of the ground floor which accompanies this paper) made between the main entrance lobby B and the attendant's room I? Was E necessary? Might not the room I have been prolonged towards the south and the lobby E omitted?

The following may be an explanation:—Supposing that there was danger of an enemy forcing an entrance at A, then the inner door C would be barred. If an enemy effected an entrance into B, they would find the defenders attacking them on the one side through the door K, whilst other defenders would attack them on the other side through the door D. Here the defenders would have the right arm free to use the sword as they came from H round E to D. This would make the door D more easily defended than the great door C, which might always be kept barred, and only used occasionally to admit stores. The doorway C has the height of 7 feet $5\frac{1}{2}$ inches to the point of the arch, and is 4 feet $10\frac{1}{2}$ inches in width. The doorway D has the height of 5 feet $8\frac{3}{4}$ inches, and width of 3 feet 2 inches.

Within a few feet of the northern side of the castle are the remains of a building of two storeys 64 feet by 22 feet 4 inches, the eastern wall of which is of similar masonry to that of the castle, as also was the northern gable. The latter, however, was removed a few years ago. The lower storey may have been a stable; it has been used as such for a long time. On the upper storey a fireplace was found in the northern gable when it was removed.

RENAISSANCE DOORWAY.

32

BELSAY CASTLE.

A residence was built against the western wall of the castle, and covering the entrance, at apparently an early date. Over its Renaissance doorway is the inscription, " Thomas Middleton and Dorathy his wife builded this house 1614." Internal evidence shows, however, that this porch was added in front of an older building, part of the southern wall of which still remains. It is to be observed that the stones with which this wall is built are more nearly square than oblong, a peculiarity also of the building of the castle. They might have been the stones of the barmkin wall taken down and used for the purpose, or there may have been a barbican opposite the entrance, and its stones may have been used.

COAT-OF-ARMS
OVER DOORWAY.

33

BELSAY CASTLE.

Underneath the above inscription and date is a shield bearing *Quarterly, first and fourth quarterly in the first quarter a cross flory* (for Middleton), *second and third crusilly of cross crosslets, three covered cups* (for Strivelyn); Crest, *A savage man holding a tree.** Below the shield are the initials, T.M. 1629.

When Hodgson was writing his History of Northumberland there then existed the remains of an armorial shield over the uppermost window on the south side of the castle, which he read as bearing the arms of Middleton impaling those of Strivelyn.†

This was, however, doubtful, as the stone was then much perished, and now there is no trace of it left; rain and frost have destroyed its face. It is probable, however, that the shield of 1629 of Middleton quartering Strivelyn was deduced from it.

It may be interesting to observe that in the old manorial times there would not be so many large timber trees and woods around the castle, much of the land being then arable, and from the battlements its cultivation by the villeins could be seen and their work superintended.

An approximate date of the building of the castle may yet possibly be formed by the collation of the masons' marks on the Northumbrian castles. The sandstone of Belsay varies in hardness, and some of the stones with which the castle is built are

---

* The workman had not left sufficient room for the savage man to be represented in an erect position, as he ought to have been, so he reduced him to a kneeling one.

† Hodgson's History of Northumberland, Part II, Vol. I, p. 359.

34

William Twopeny: Porch to seventeenth-century house.

Masons' Marks.	ⅎ	ⅎ	¥	朩	丮	⅄	++	4	⊣	𝚪
Two Turret vaults, the south-western and the north-eastern................................										
Upper part of staircase above door of clock room							3			
Staircase wall at level of clock room................					14				1	
Clock room................................		1			7					
Staircase wall at level of great hall, and chapel wall................................		4							3	
Top room above entresole, north-western corner		3		1	9					
Room above entresole, north-west corner..........									7	
Room above the great hall..............................	4	12	8	5	95					
Chapel..										
Great hall, above the fourth course................								1	8	1
Outsides of outer walls above the offset............		1		1		2				
Great hall, the first four courses above the floor								2		
Entresole, north-western corner										
Entresole, vault opening off stair										
Little vault under stair										
Attendant's vault in basement......................										
Little lobby to attendant's vault in basement.....										
Entrance lobby......................................										
Large vault in basement										
Outsides of outer walls below offset										
TOTALS............	4	21	8	7	125	2	3	3	19	1

BELSAY CASTLE.

]	I	⊓	⋔	⊕	○	<	⊠	†	✕✕	✳	+	⊀	⟋	Z	⌇	W	→	TOTALS.
											7		1					8
			1	8								22						34
				11						1		9						36
				5								5						18
	2	2	1	2	6	1							8			1		30
				11						2		15	2					43
	3	8	7	3	47			2				2	31	3	4	3	1	121
				61			3	2			1	149	1		1			343
3	4	2	5	1	18	1				2			13	2	1	2	5	59
2	3	10	17	5	51					4	1		49	3	2	3	3	164
		1	1	2	13						1		12	1	2	3	1	42
					10	1			1	4	1	1	6	10	22	9	6	74
					2				2	10	1		1	5	9	8	11	49
					1				2	2	1			2	4	2	3	17
									8	2	1		10		3	1	16	41
									1		1		4		5	7	33	51
									1		1				1	4	3	10
									5		1				1		4	11
					3	2			5	2	7	6	29	1	18	21	79	173
					9				4	5	2	7	10	3	25	31	105	201
5	12	23	32	110	160	7	7		29	32	23	216	178	31	97	96	270	1525

much decayed by the weather, whilst others still show the original faces. Fortunately, at about 20 feet from the ground level, a moulded offset forms a dripstone, which has given further protection to the stones below, and several marks can be seen, whilst above the offset the stones are much more decayed, and fewer marks remain. Many stones, though their faces are not decayed, do not show a mark; it is possible that their marks, if any, are on their joints or beds. The accompanying chart shows all the marks now visible throughout the castle; a few are still hidden from view by the plaster carrying the remains of the mural decorations, and others are in inaccessible positions. Below the offset the marks most frequently occurring, both outside and inside the castle, are w, ⟩, ⟨, and ⤢. About the time that the building reached the level where the offset moulding was placed, a considerable change seems to have taken place in the staff of builders, both inside and outside, w and ⟩, who had hitherto done so much work, soon disappear, ⤢ remains and works on the level of the great hall, and ⟨ and ⋏, who had done a little work below the offset, do much work in the upper storeys. ◯, ⋔, and ⤴ begin above the offset, whilst ⨎ and several varieties of this mark do not begin till the uppermost storey is well advanced. This change in the staff of the builders seems to indicate a period of cessation of the work. It has been suggested above, that Sir John de Strivelyn, to whom the grant of Belsay was made in 1335, may have commenced the building. Should he have done so before 1348, such a cessation would be likely to take place on the outbreak of the Great

35

Plague or Black Death in that year, and several years might have elapsed before the building was resumed. A thick line has been drawn across the chart of masons' marks where approximately the cessation may have taken place. The masons using the marks w, ⇀, ⌇, and others, may have left a few stones ready dressed, with their marks upon them, and these may have been worked into the building by the new staff; others, such as ⨍, and ⊹, may have survived the plague, and then continued their work on the recommencement of the building.

AN 18TH CENTURY GATEWAY.

36

BELSAY CASTLE IN 1819.

APPENDIX.

REMAINS OF ANCIENT MURAL PAINTINGS IN BELSAY CASTLE.

Report of Mr. B. M. Leach *of the Firm of Messrs. F. R. Leach & Sons, St. Mary's Passage, Cambridge.*

I have made a careful and thorough examination of these remains, which, from the character of the work, I attribute to the 15th century. Unfortunately, from their fragmentary nature, and the absence of any distinctive costume, it is difficult to assign the date with any great accuracy: yet the process employed, the well-known one of " fresco," points to their execution soon after the building was completed.

Without question, the hall was completely covered with paintings on the upper wall, the lower part being probably hung with arras, afterwards replaced by panelling. I find indistinct traces of figures in several places.

There are indications of two distinct paintings on the window splays, the first consisting of an outline pattern in red and black, very little of which now remains, and the second of a somewhat more elaborate character.

37

The principal remains are on the south wall on the eastern side of the window, and consist of two parts. The upper depicts some naval scene, painted in the usual brown outline colour on the plaster. The only other colour in this portion is an ochreous brown, with which the hulls and masts of the ships are painted, with no attempt by hatching or otherwise to represent light or shade. There is, moreover, no attempt to indicate water surface, which is somewhat rare. The lower part must have been a fine piece of colour when executed. The ground, I have no doubt, was green (probably somewhat brighter than that of the drawing sent herewith), diapered with clusters of tiny white flowers having red centres.

On this background stood, at more or less regular intervals, tree trunks, with both roots and branches displayed, but lopped off, suggesting the celebrated " Ragged Staff." These are painted a brick red, outlined with white, and " high lighted " by white hatching. On some of these trees are hung shields, three of which remain with armorial bearings upon them. It may be that these shields bore the arms of various families connected by marriage or otherwise with the owner of the Castle, or possibly one of the numerous confraternities of the middle ages was accustomed to meet here, and the shields bore the arms of its members. Again the insufficiency of the remains forbids more than vague speculation.

On the western half of the south wall I discovered faint traces of two angels, painted in outline with great delicacy. And on the east wall I found indications of a figure in a red robe, which was probably at least four feet high. Nothing definite is left of the figure excepting the left arm, which is placed " akimbo."

On the upper north wall of the north-east corner I found traces of similar treatment to that of the south wall, but nothing is left beyond a shield (sable, a saltire argent), and faint traces of the " tree trunk " painting. Round the north window was a stencilled border, a portion of which, full size, I have drawn.

On that part of the wall, at the south end, which was probably hung with arras, I find traces of a check pattern in black, grey, and white (also figured half-size). This, I should say, must have been painted considerably later than the upper wall—possibly even as late as the 17th century.

The window splays, as before remarked, have certainly been decorated on two occasions, the second painting being, I think, not much later than the first. All the details, as far as possible, I have copied. They present no striking peculiarities beyond that they were all, without exception, stencilled.

It has afforded me great pleasure to examine and copy these quaint and interesting specimens of mediæval art, and I can only once more express my regret that so large a proportion has disappeared, and my pleasure at being able to preserve some memorial of the few fragments remaining.

THE END.

*Watercolours in various hands
from an album which belonged to
Lady Mary Monck (née Tankerville)
second wife of Sir Charles Monck*

about 1830.

Belsay Castle as it is.

4 ½

F. M.

GLOSSARY OF TERMS USED IN AN ACCOUNT OF BELSAY CASTLE

ARRAS, a kind of tapestry from Arras in the department of Pas-de-Calais in the north of France.

ASHLAR (a word of French derivation). Stones hewn and squared. They are usually set in regular courses as the facing to a wall, and the work is called ashlar-work. When the stones unhewn and rough as they come from the quarry are placed irregularly in the wall, the work is called rubble-work or rough-walling.

ASPHALT. The kind called Vol-de-Seyssel is made from a bituminous limestone found near Seyssel in the department of Ain in the East of France.

BARBICAN (French, *Barbacane*), usually applied to an advanced building for defending the entrance to a fortification, castle etc, as before the gate or the drawbridge.

BARMKIN, see PEEL.

BATTLEMENT, see PARAPET.

BRETESCHE, a wooden roofed erection pierced with loop-holes and machicolated (see MACHICOLATION), placed on the upper parts of fortifications for purposes of defence, or used for attack on the walls by the party below.

CAMBERED BEAM, a beam slightly curved upwards so that it is slightly arched. They are used in roofs. See drawing, p. 16.

CAP-MOULDING, see COPING (see the South Battlement).

CINQUEFOIL, see FOIL.

COPING, the covering course of a wall or battlement. It may be flat, or moulded to throw off rainwater, or have a roll moulding on the top to stop the course of arrows from below. It is sometimes called capping or, when moulded, a CAP-MOULDING

43

CORBEL, a piece of stone projecting out from the face of a wall to carry any superincumbent weight, as a parapet etc.

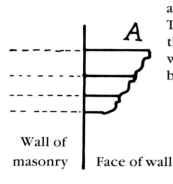

a corbel formed of three oversailing stones. These stones are very long, and are built into the wall, so that the set of corbels may bear a weight placed upon it at A, as for instance, a battlement. See the drawing under CAPMOULDING.

Wall of masonry | Face of wall

CUSP, see FOIL.

DEXTRAL, relating to the right hand.

EMBRASURE, see PARAPET.

FOIL, from the French *feuille*, any small arc in the tracery of a Gothic arch or panel. The projecting points of intersection of the arcs or foils are called CUSPS, Latin *cuspis* a point; and the work treated is said to have trefoil or cinque-foil etc cusping. See drawing on p. 16.

HOOD-MOULDING, see MOULD.

LOOP or LOOP-HOLE, a narrow opening in a wall for the discharge of arrows etc, or for the purpose of a look-out or window for ventilation.

MACHICOLATIONS (from the French *mâchicoulis* or *mâchecoulis*), a term used in modern descriptions of military architecture, where they mean openings formed by setting a parapet outwards on corbels so as to project beyond the face of the wall, the intervals between the corbels being left open to allow missiles such as stones etc. to be thrown down on assailants.

The derivation of the French word *mâchicoulis* does not seem to be accurately known. It appears to be *mâché*, mashed or crushed matter from *mâcher* (as *mâchefer* the scales from hammered iron, or the waste slag from an iron furnace) and *coulis* in medieval French meaning a sliding or pouring. The two garderobes shown in the plans of Belsay

44

GLOSSARY OF TERMS

Castle following page 16 are in the chimney-looking erection seen in the photo of the north side of the castle opposite page 12 and are supported on three corbels and thus are machicolated giving one *mâchicoulis* to each garderobe. Unfortunately the machicolation comes just behind the eaves of the roof of the outbuilding seen in the photograph and is therefore not shown. There is a space of about 10 feet between the outbuilding and the Castle into which the refuse from the garderobes must have fallen. It seems not improbable that the term *mâchicoulis* arose in domestic life. Many old houses had an upper storey corbelled outwork over the lower storey and it would be a convenience to pour ashes and house-dirt through a hole in the floor over any one or more of the spaces between the corbels. So also in a Castle the household refuse, rushes in quantity from the floors etc would be put down the nearest garderobe *mâchicoulis*. 'Put it down the *mâchicoulis*' must have been a term in common use.

When the *mâchicoulis* were built as part of the defensive parapet on the top of a castle, which was not till the 13th century, the word *mâchicoulis* was ready for use, and in later times when the improved state of the towns forbade the use of domestic *mâchicoulis* the word remained as a term of military architecture only.

MERLON, see under PARAPET.

MOULD, in architecture is a model, templet or pattern used by workmen as a guide in working the varieties of outline or contour given to the angles of projections or cavities, such as cornices, window-jambs, dripstones or hood-mouldings over windows etc. The mould consists of a thin wooden board or plate of metal cut to represent the exact section of the moulding that is to be worked from it.

> HOOD-MOULDING, the projecting moulding over the heads of arches, windows etc, also called a dripstone. See over windows on south wall.

MULLION, a vertical post dividing a window into lights, a corruption from the Old English munnion, from the French *moignon* a stump.

> See TRANSOM.

NEWEL, the vertical cylindrical column round which the steps of a spiral stair wind. See Plate opp. p. 18.

GLOSSARY OF TERMS

OFF-SET, the part of a wall which is exposed horizontally when the portion of the wall above it is reduced in thickness. If a moulded stone such as a dripstone be placed upon the off-set it is called a moulded off-set.

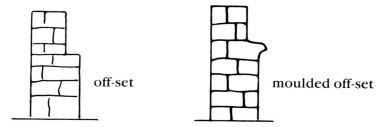

off-set   moulded off-set

OVERSAIL, to project beyond the general face. See CORBEL.

PARAPET (from the Italian *parapetto*, from *parare* to protect, and *petto* the breast). A low wall raised breast high upon the ramparts and other military structures, for defence against missiles from without.

> BATTLEMENT, a notched or indented parapet employed in fortifications consisting of a series of rising parts called MERLONS separated by open spaces called EMBRASURES or CRENELLES.

PEEL or PELE (from the Old French *Pel* or *Pal*, a stake or pale, and that from the Latin *palus*, a stake.

In early English times, a peel was a fortified enclosure made as a place of defence and shelter for men, cattle and goods by forming around it a rampart of earth strengthened by heavy timber and crowned with a palisade. A fortified house was built within the peel for the use of its defenders. The construction of earth and timber decayed away and the house, which in later times was built of stone, remaining, retained the name of 'Peel'. In Northumberland the word peel is little used. The larger towers (turres) such as Belsay, Chipchase and Bywell, are usually called by the natives castles or towers, rarely Peels. Horton Peel, about 2½ miles south-west of Blyth, was constructed in the later years of the 13th century, and was formed by an earthen rampart and moat enclosing a space measuring 203 feet by 190 feet, within which was a crenellated dwelling house. See Northumberland volume of the *Victoria County History* for illustration.

46

GLOSSARY OF TERMS

A BARMKIN was more modern than a peel, but served the same purpose viz. that of a defence and shelter. The rampart of a barmkin was built of stone and lime and thus differed from that of a peel which was made of earth and timber. It was built around an existing house or tower or was contemporaneous with it, the tower being sometimes of more importance than the barmkin, whereas the peel was of more importance than its house or tower. The word is probably derived from 'berm', a space of vacant ground along the inside of a rampart.

PLINTH, a projecting face at the bottom of a wall immediately above the surface of the ground, usually moulded on its upper surface as is usually seen on the wooden skirting round a room.

ROOF-TREE, the beam forming the ridge of a roof, into which the upper ends of them rafters are fixed.

SARKING, thin boarding covering the rafters of a roof, on which lead or slates are laid. So called in the North of England. In the South it is called slate-boarding.

SEGMENTAL STONES, see VOUSSOIR.

SINISTRAL, relating to the left hand.

SOFFIT (from the French *Soffite*). The under surface of a ceiling, arch, window-head, horizontal beam or other architectural feature.

SQUINT, an oblique opening passing through the wall of a church for the purpose of enabling persons in the transepts or aisles to see the altar.

TINCTURE, the name given in Heraldry to the colours used, including gold and silver and the furs as ermines etc.

TRANSOM, a horizontal mullion or cross-bar in a window, dividing it into stages or heights. See window of Great Hall, p. 16.

TREFOIL, see FOIL.

TURRET (from the Old French *tourette*, diminutive of *tour*).

A small tower, especially at the angles of larger buildings, sometimes partly over-sailing and built on corbels as at Belsay.

TYMPANUM (from an old form *typanon* with an 'm' inserted, the part of a drum which is struck, from a Greek word *typto* to strike, and so came to be applied to the stretched top of a drum).

GLOSSARY OF TERMS

In Architecture the term is applied to a vertical flat surface or space, usually triangular (but not always so), surmounting an architectural feature as in the pediment or gable of a Greek temple.

Thus where two or more smaller arches are grouped together under one larger one as in the windows of the Great Hall at Belsay, a blank space or tympanum is created; on the exterior, between the hood-mould and the heads of the two arches (see south wall); on the interior, between the soffit of the larger arch and the heads of the two smaller arches (see drawing, p. 16).

VOUSSOIR or ARCH-STONE, a stone cut in the form of a truncated wedge or section of a curved figure, with a series of which an arch is constructed.

The voussoirs of the arches of the doorways in the castle at Belsay are so long in the line of the circumference of the curve, a single stone sometimes forming one half of the arch, that they are not true arch-stones and are better described as SEGMENTAL STONES.

arch of voussoirs   a Belsay doorway

The arch formed with   a truncated
two segmental stones   wedge